INTERRUPTING ANXIETY

Practical Tools to Help Interrupt Anxious Thoughts

By

Lianne Weaver

The information in this book is not intended to replace the advice of a physician or other medical professional. You should consult a medical professional in matters relating to health, especially if you have existing medical conditions, and before starting, stopping, or changing the dose of any medication you are taking. Individual readers are solely responsible for their own health-care decisions. The author and the publisher do not accept responsibility for any adverse effects individuals may claim to experience, whether directly or indirectly, from the information contained in this book.

This book is dedicated to my husband Tom and daughter Seren, who have always believed in me, even when I haven't believed in myself.

Table of Contents

Introduction   6

Part I: What is Anxiety?   11

Chapter One:

    General Symptoms of Anxiety   15

Chapter Two:

    Stress, Worry and Anxiety   23

Chapter Three:

    Anxiety Disorders   31

Part II: Managing Anxiety   37

Chapter Four:

    How to Manage Your Anxiety   37

Chapter Five:

    How to Help Someone With

    Anxiety   53

Chapter Six:

    Panic Attacks   61

Conclusion   71

Further Resources   76

Acknowledgements   79

About The Author   81

Introduction

Congratulations on taking your first step to manage and control those anxious thoughts! Right about now, your anxious voice is probably cynically expecting very little from this book however, I will let you in on a little secret (lean in!) what you are about to learn works and will give you tools to use for a lifetime to help interrupt (and maybe even silence from time to time) that anxious voice.

Before we get into content, lets cover some of the basics to help you get the most out of this book and also to ensure that anxious voice does not take over.

1. Take notes – Really! I know this is a short book but that does not make its content any less powerful or impactful. Very few of us can recall everything we read once and if all you do is read this book once, the chances are you will forget a lot of it within a few days. When you make notes, you are ensuring your brain is more actively involved in the learning process and so you are far more likely to retain what we cover. To supercharge this, don't make digital notes but turn to good old fashioned pen and paper!

2. Pause – As a short eBook the temptation may be to consume it all in one sitting, but there will be exercises and opportunities for reflection so take an opportunity to pause and digest what is covered.

3. There is no magic pill – Everyone is different, our mental and emotional experiences are different, how we learn is different and our beliefs are different. That means that, unfortunately, I cannot give a one size fits all approach to any wellbeing, mental health or personal development topic. However, what I can do is offer a wide variety of tools and techniques with the intention that at least one of them will work for you.

4. One sit up doesn't create a six pack – On the topic of magic pills, doing these exercises once will unfortunately not yield permanent results just as one sit up does not make a six pack (darn it!). You may not notice changes initially but have faith that you are teaching your brain to respond in a different way and eventually the commitment to that will show positive results.

5. All experiences are different – As pointed out, we are all different and thus anxiety and all mental health issues can manifest in different ways. Don't compare yourself to others and don't worry that you may

have different experiences to them. If you are at all concerned about how you are managing your anxiety, please seek help from the support services listed in this book.

6. Don't procrastinate – So often, we flick through a book and buy it with optimism of learning the secrets to life and then we leave it on a bookshelf (or on our eBook reader, for years and years). As much as I believe in the tools in this book being powerful, not one of them is powerful enough to work if you do not even read it! Procrastination is something anxious people do quite well (when the world is scary, it often feels safer to do nothing) so do not let it prevent you from making these positive changes.

7. Use the Resources – Within this book you will find some exercises, if you would rather complete them as worksheets, we have a range of resources available for you to download. All you need to do it scan the QR code at the end of the book or visit https://www.beamtraining.co.uk/beamresources and you will be able to access them.

Now you have an idea of how to get the most out of this book let's have a look at what we will be covering. We will begin with getting a better understanding of what anxiety really is, it's something every human is familiar with and yet not every human struggles with it. We will also look at some of the common symptoms of anxiety and look at how it can vary widely from individual to individual.

Importantly, we will begin to look at how to manage anxiety. Where I will share with you some of my favourite tools that I have used in therapy sessions and training sessions with clients.

I'll also give you some tips to help someone with anxiety, many of us love people who struggle with anxiety and that can be scary, you might think I don't know what to do, I don't know what to say to them, I don't know how to handle it. We will therefore learn specific tools to help support others from our children to colleagues.

We will also look at panic attacks, you won't necessarily have a panic attack if you have anxiety, but they do frequently go together, it is therefore really important that we understand what a panic attack is, again for ourselves and if we're around someone else having one we can understand why those panic attacks arise. Importantly we will also cover some brilliant tools and techniques for managing those panic attacks.

Finally, I will also give you some information on where you can get some further help and support.

Part I: What is Anxiety?

Anxiety is a normal part of being a human being. Every single person has experienced anxiety at some point, it could be feeling anxious for a test, for an upcoming job interview or for a first date; all of us will have an awareness of what anxiety can feel like. It exists to let us know that there is something out of the normal ahead of us and it ensures we are as prepared as possible for it. We could also think of anxiety as showing us that we care about something, we are far more likely to feel anxious over a job interview we really want than one we could not stand to do.

As a human, our species needs anxiety, it has been considered to be a really normal and essential part of being a human being. Some philosophers, such as Sartre believed that anxiety gave us indications on whether our choices were good for us or whether they were harmful for us. However, Sigmund Freud, argued that anxiety was central to a host of other psychological disorders, suggesting that anxiety was a sign that there was something not right, and anxiety was more of a negative experience.

11

Now, our views today have definitely evolved. Anxiety is something that we talk about on a regular basis, but it is still something that feels hard to define and something that can have a lot of confusion around it. One of the main reasons for this is because the criteria for diagnosing anxiety is changing frequently.

The other real big challenge is that no one can be a complete expert of the human condition, because we all have our own human experience. Anxiety, for me may look very different to your own experience of anxiety, which can make it really difficult for us to really categorize it and pigeonhole it. In its positive form, anxiety is there to prepare us for potentially a novel situation, difficult situation or dangerous situation.

The Psychological Association definition of anxiety is "an emotion characterized by feelings of tension, worrying thoughts, or physical changes, such as an increase in your blood pressure".

But anxiety can vary in its severity. And for some of us, it can be something that can impact every moment of our life and be really debilitating.

For some of us anxiety is persistent, frequent, and it can be so overwhelming that it can cause us to make even the smallest decision, a massive issue for us, making it difficult for us to even complete the most simple of tasks.

And because we're all unique, our experiences are unique. However, we do know that anxiety becomes more of an issue when it is prolonged.

In the most generalist terms, we can say that anxiety moves into becoming an issue when it ticks all three of these boxes:

- It is long lasting

- It impacts our work and / or relationships

- It frequently impacts our physical and / or mental health

Throughout the rest of this book, we will look at what we really mean when we talk about anxiety impacting our physical and / or mental health and look more into how the experience of anxiety can differ and be defined.

Chapter One: General Symptoms of Anxiety

If we know that everyone can experience anxiety differently, it is useful to recognise some of the generalised symptoms of anxiety knowing that we will not necessarily experience all or every symptom, but we can develop an understanding of how anxiety can impact ourselves and others.

Anxiety will impact us in three main ways; physically, psychologically and behaviourally and each of these can overlap.

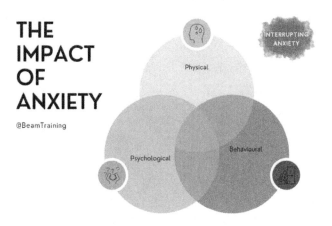

THE IMPACT OF ANXIETY

@BeamTraining

Physical

Psychological

Behavioural

Physical Symptoms of Anxiety

Anxiety is usually a very physical experience. When we feel anxious, we may feel shaky, or become more aware of our heartbeat, we may begin to breathe faster, sweat or get a dry mouth. All of these are caused by the brain's stress response being triggered in order to essentially prepare us to 'fight or flight'. Some of the typical physical symptoms are:

- Palpitations
- Rapid heartbeat
- Flushing
- Shortness of breath
- Dizziness
- Sweating
- Tingling

- Dry mouth
- Nausea
- Frequent trips to the bathroom
- Shaking
- Headaches
- Aches and pains

Exercise

Make a list of some of the physical symptoms you feel when you feel anxious (It is useful to begin to be able to recognise that these physical responses are all signs of your experience of anxiety).

When I feel anxious, I experience these physical symptoms:

Psychological Symptoms of Anxiety

Anxiety changes how we think and can cause us to believe that there are threats everywhere. When we are in the grips of anxiety, we may feel we have no control over our thoughts, worries and negative thinking. Some of the psychological symptoms of anxiety are:

17

- Excessive fear or worrying
- Mind racing
- Mind going blank
- Inability to concentrate
- Irritability

- Catastrophic thinking
- Confusion
- Tiredness
- Intrusive thoughts
- Restlessness
- Feeling on edge

Exercise

Make a list of some of the psychological symptoms you experience when you feel anxious (It is useful to begin to be able to recognise that these responses are all signs of your experience of anxiety).

When I feel anxious, I experience these psychological symptoms:

Behavioural Symptoms of Anxiety

When we experience anxiety, it can make us behave in a way we would never normally behave. It may mean that we're short tempered with our loved ones, we withdraw from social situations or that we are irritable. Some of the behavioural symptoms of anxiety are:

- Avoiding situations
- Repetitive compulsive behaviour
- Distress in social situations
- Urges to escape situations
- Discomfort
- Withdrawing from others
- Excessively people pleasing
- Over analysing what others may think

Exercise

Make a list of some of the behavioural symptoms you experience when you feel anxious (It is useful to begin to be able to recognise that these responses are all signs of your experience of anxiety).

When I feel anxious, I behave this way:

As we can see, anxiety has many ways in which it can impact us and essentially these changes all come down to our brains being a heightened state of fear and trepidation for a potentially dangerous future event.

If you were about to abseil down a building for the first time, it is likely you would have a racing heart, be breathing fast, have sweaty palms, feel on edge, have some thoughts of things going badly wrong, wonder why you are doing it and want to escape … and many more responses too. This makes sense, our brain knows we have a potentially threatening situation up ahead and triggers the amygdala within the limbic region of the brain. The amygdala is our fear centre which is the part of the brain that prepares us for that fight or flight response, it makes us hyper aware of threats, causes us to be able to respond really quickly and causes us to have tunnel vision of the threat. All of these are pretty useful in our abseiling example, it is useful to be hyper focused and not distracted. However, when we struggle with anxiety, our brain receives the same threatening messages even when rationally, we know that there is no threatening situation up ahead. Even so, the survival part of our brain (the limbic region in which the amygdala sits) will respond even if you rationally know that you are not in a life or death situation. This part of the brain is far more dominant when we feel threatened and will trigger the physiological response of stress throughout your body and mind, it then becomes impossible for our rational thoughts to calm it down.

Key Takeaways

- Not everyone experiences anxiety in the same way

- Anxiety impacts us in three main ways, physically, psychologically and behaviourally

- We are impacted in these three ways due to the brain believing we are about to face a threatening situation

- The amygdala is often known as the part of the brain which triggers the 'fight or flight' response

- Whenever we feel threatened our survival brain will override our rational thinking

In the next chapter, you will learn...

The differences between stress, worry and anxiety which are often used synonymously and are often difficult to differentiate from when experienced.

Chapter Two: Stress, Worry and Anxiety

If you struggle with anxiety, then there is a good chance you will also know what it is like to feel stressed or to worry. Whilst the three conditions are different, they often go hand in hand and it is sometimes impossible to see where one begins and one ends. Whilst we will not be going into a huge amount of detail about worry and stress in this book, we do have additional resources and eBooks on both topics.

Stress

As we are already becoming more informed on anxiety, let's begin by looking at stress.

Stress is the normal psychological and physiological response to a real or perceived threat, it is something every single human being experiences and has been an essential part of our survival.

Stress is not necessarily a bad thing, we need to feel stress in order to motivate us to take urgent action. In its most primate form, stress is what has enabled humans to survive, being alert and aware of any physical threats ensured we survived wars, famine, floods and more. However, stress is not only experienced when we are physically threatened but stress occurs any time we feel emotionally threatened too, for example attending a job interview, public speaking or even someone criticising us. Rationally we know these are not life threatening situations but as we have already learned, the part of the brain that is always keeping us safe does not work on rational thought and so we will often respond to these situations with stress.

What is even more interesting about our stress response is that we not only become stressed when under real threat, but we can simply think about something threatening and the brain will respond as if it is really happening. Lying awake at 3am thinking of a difficult conversation with your boss which may or may not ever happen makes you feel as stressed as if it was really happening.

In our modern world, the danger with the stress we now experience, is that due to us becoming stressed over fewer tangible threats than being chased by a lion, we can remain in chronic stress, this is when stress can become detrimental to our physical and mental health.

If we are in a state of chronic stress, it is likely that we will overthink the threat causing us to worry about it and also become anxious about what may or may not happen.

Worry

Whilst we can have a physiological response to worry (a knot in our stomach for example), worry begins as a form of thinking and again, not all worry is bad. Worrying can be useful and show us where we need to focus our energy for example, you begin to worry about an exam you have next week. This not only indicates that you care about the outcome, but it also can motivate you to knuckle down and do some more revision.

We can think of worrying as our brains problem solving tool. When we present our brain with a tricky problem, it will resort to worrying as a way of coming up with the most appropriate solution. When the problem is then solved, we no longer need to worry. This is useful worrying as it enables us to be creative and find a solution we may not have previously seen or thought of.

Useful Worrying

Worry Starts
You start worrying and think of possible solutions and outcomes

The Problem
A warning light flashes on your car whilst on the motorway

Solution
You see a service station up ahead and safely pull into it for assistance

@BeamTraining

In the example shown, worrying leads to us considering who we could call, if we have breakdown cover, if there is a garage or service station ahead etc. Once we have solved that initial problem, the worry cycle is complete, the brain has done its job and we no longer need to be in a state of worry.

However, worrying becomes problematic when we give the brain a problem it cannot solve. These are usually problems which are far outside our ability to control such as global issues or other people's behaviours.

When we begin to worry about problems we cannot solve, the brain will still see the problem presented as something to fix but in its powerless within that situation, it will never be able to come to the solution and complete that worry process causing us to be trapped in a worry loop.

Let's imagine that you receive a phone call that your uncle needs an operation, you instantly receive this information as a problem that needs to be solved and so your brain resorts to worrying to come up with solutions. Unfortunately, assuming you are not the appropriate surgeon, this problem is outside of your ability to control it and so you remain worrying.

The problem is that we often worry about things we have no control over, which makes us feel more out of control, therefore more stressed, therefore more anxious. This can create a loop where these three different really consuming emotional states start to manifest together.

Exercise

Write a list of everything you are worried about right now. Then identify if this is something you can control or cannot. Focus your attention on the worries you can control and decide to take action towards resolving them. You may find you are worried about some issues which you can partially control but not fully, break them down and again focus upon where your control lies.

Things I am worried about:	Can I control this?	
	Yes	No

Key Takeaways

- Worry, stress and anxiety are three different states which can often feed into each other.

- Stress is a normal physiological and psychological response to a real or perceived threat.

- Stress when triggered due to a physical threat is usually very helpful.

- Stress when triggered due to an emotional threat is usually unhelpful and can lead to chronic stress.

- Worry is a way in which the brain tries to problem solve.

- Some worries are useful to inspire us to be creative and come up with solutions.

- Worrying becomes problematic when we worry about things outside of our control and get caught in a worry loop.

In the next chapter, you will learn…

About different anxiety disorders as classified by the UK charity MIND.

Chapter Three: Anxiety Disorders

As we have already discussed, anxiety can be a very subjective experience and can be difficult to define. However, an anxiety disorder is usually defined when do not experience what would be considered a 'normal' reaction to a situation, when our response may be considered to be out of proportion compared to how others would respond in the same situation, for example we may have an exaggerated response, extreme negative thoughts and / or excessive intrusive thoughts.

This book is in no way here to help you diagnose anxiety disorders, this should only be done with your GP or mental health professional. However, according to the UK Mental Health charity MIND, there are currently eight anxiety disorders which it is useful to be aware of.

Generalized Anxiety Disorder, or GAD

This is the most common form of anxiety disorder often defined by an excessive worrying over very nonspecific life events, objects, situations. GAD can be very different from person to person but the key word to GAD is that *excessive*, excessive worry, defined by more than what would normally be expected.

Panic Disorder

We will discuss panic attacks later on in this book, but a panic disorder is defined by sudden attacks of intense emotion, terror and apprehension. This can be horrific for the sufferer, because sometimes they can seemingly come out of the blue and so sometimes people with a panic disorder, fear the panic, more than anything else. This creates more anxiety about having another panic attack and it becomes a really horrible, vicious circle.

Phobias

Something that is not often considered when we think about it as an anxiety disorder, is a phobia. A phobia is an irrational fear, or an avoidance of something that can be all consuming. So phobias are very different to regular fears or dislikes. Everyone has fears, but we can usually function around that fear. A phobia, however, can make us absolutely incapable of functioning at the same time as causing feelings of anxiety to escalate.

Social Anxiety

An anxiety disorder that is becoming increasingly common, not least because of our experience over the last few years, is social anxiety. Social anxiety disorder causes the sufferer to be anxious about social situations. This could be due to lots of reasons such as fear of being judged, rejected, embarrassed, humiliated, not fitting in, other people talking about us etc.

Post Traumatic Stress Disorder (PTSD also now known as Post Traumatic Stress Injury – PTSI)

PTSD/I develops when we have gone through a traumatic experience. We often think of a traumatic experience of needing to be this great, big, catastrophic event that has happened in our lives, which of course can be the case such as when soldiers return from war. However, we can experience PTSD/I from any event that we interpreted as traumatic at the time, due to this, some people do not seek help for their PTSD/I considering their event not 'big' enough to justify their response. The truth is, it doesn't really matter what the event was, the trauma comes from our response to the event.

Health Anxiety

Becoming overly concerned with being ill or even interacting with something that could make us ill can cause some of us to experience health anxiety. This can cause the sufferer to obsess over symptoms and over focus upon their health.

34

Body Dysmorphic Disorder (BDD)

BDD is when we excessively worry, or obsess about our physical appearance in some way, causing us to see something that other people might not even see in us. We might obsess over a certain body part not looking the way we think it should or we may feel ashamed of how we look. We literally have a dysmorphic view of ourselves. It can lead to unhealthy eating habits, to unhealthy treatment of ourselves, being obsessed with diet and exercise, cosmetic surgery, etc.

Perinatal Anxiety or Perinatal OCD

This usually develops either when someone is pregnant, or within about the first year of giving birth. Whilst it is normal for a new mum to feel anxious when pregnant and with a new baby, this is far more excessive anxious and obsessive behaviour that can intrude in their enjoyment of being pregnant or being with their new born.

If you are experiencing anxiety, which is negatively affecting your daily life, if you feel that the anxiety you're experiencing is excessive, or if you suspect you've got one of these conditions, I urge you to take this as your sign to say, today is the day I'm going to talk to someone. We have lots of support references for you at the end of this book.

Key Takeaways

- According to MIND there are currently eight types of anxiety disorder

- It is important not to self diagnose and to seek professional help if you believe you have an anxiety disorder.

In the next chapter, you will learn...

How to begin to manage your own anxiety with five key tools.

Part II – Managing Anxiety

Chapter Four: How to Manage Your Anxiety

With a greater understanding of anxiety, we can now begin to look at tools to help you manage periods of anxiety within your life.

Talk To Someone

Remember when you were young, you were laying in the dark trying to sleep and you convinced yourself that there was a monster under your bed, you lay there frozen in fear, convinced you hear something and maybe even that you have seen a flash of something moving. As you lay there in the dark becoming more and more scared, the 'monster' becomes more and more terrifying. Eventually, you pluck up the courage to put your torch on and look around the room, the scary shadows you saw were a coat on the back of the chair, the noise you heard was your radiator, the light helps you put everything into perspective and bring your fear back down.

When we struggle with negative, anxious or fearful thoughts, they 'grow' larger when we keep them to ourselves, however if we can share our fears with someone we suddenly get perspective and realise that many were unfounded and not as scary as we first thought. I call this is the 'monster under your bed effect'.

Although talking to someone may be the most daunting tool I share for some readers, the reality is whenever we keep any mental health issue to ourselves it often grows and becomes worse.

If you feel that anxiety is impacting you, and you feel that, maybe this is a bit more than being just a bit nervous, then I urge you to talk to someone you trust. The key part of choosing to talk to someone is choosing the right person to talk to. You may have an amazing friend but whenever you bring up feeling anxious, they make you feel worse by adding to it, talking about themselves or even shutting you down. To feel better, it is important we are selective in who we choose to talk to. Choosing someone who will listen well, won't try to fix things and will understand can make all the difference in us feeling more accepted.

Consider who you have that you can truly talk to, a friend, colleague, relative or professional and make sure you use their support when you need it. You will be amazed at how powerful it is when you have a safe space to let out your thoughts. It also often helps you to feel more 'normal' when you chat to someone who can explain that other people sometimes think and feel the same way too.

If you are someone that thinks that there is no way you could ever open up to someone then there is a helpful second option, write it down. Talking is great, because you can get it all out, and you can get a of third person perspective on your problems. But if that's too overwhelming, and too scary, get a pen and paper and write down every single thing that is in your head right now, this is a really good tool. The amazing power of writing things down, is you can still get a third person perspective on it because as you are writing it, you can take a step back.

It can be really liberating and insightful for you as you may not realise everything you were carrying or exactly how you were feeling until it is all set out in front of you. This can not only give you clarity, but it can also help you to see patterns in your behaviour.

Breathe

We take an average of around 25,000 breaths a day, most of which are completely passive, in that you don't usually pay attention to them. But every single breath you have already taken today (and every other day) sends a signal to your brain to let it know if you are safe, or if you are under threat, even if you are not noticing it.

Our breathing is one of the most fundamental parts of communication between our body and our brain. We know that our brain tells our body what to do, thankfully, but what we are not always aware of is the fact that our body is also telling our brain what to do (and importantly, how to feel).

That is brilliant news for anxiety sufferers, because sometimes we can't get out of our heads and simply think differently as some people may suggest, but we can change what we are doing with our body. One of the easiest ways to tap into this body / mind connection is by changing how we breathe.

Think about it, you are lying in bed at three o'clock in the morning, and all of a sudden you hear a loud bang that wakes you up, your likely initial reaction is to gasp, hold your breath and then resort into rapid breathing which all prepares your brain that you are in a potentially threatening situation, triggering the release of stress hormones, an increase in heart rate and blood pressure and many more physiological responses. You jump out of bed, you look out the window, and you see that it was caused by a cat knocking over a bin. "Phew! What a relief" you let out a sigh and gradually start to slow your breathing which in turn, assures your brain that you are safe.

We can use this information to get the body to feel more relaxed which in turn stops us feeling anxious, with three basic rules to breathing:

1. Breathe through your nose – Whenever we are stressed or anxious it is likely we are breathing through

our mouths not our noses. In fact, our mouths are our emergency breathing system and should only be used as such. Any time we breathe through our mouths, our brain is receiving a signal that we are in danger. It is our noses that are designed for breathing and when we use them to breathe not only do we get a far more efficient supply of oxygen but we also breathe deeper and signal to our brains that we are safe.

2. Breathe Slower – Whenever we are anxious we are also likely to be over breathing, the optimum breathing rate is around 5.5 breaths per minute, many of us will be breathing well over 15 breaths per minute! Again causing stress signals to be received and placing more strain on the respiratory and cardiovascular systems than necessary.

3. Exhale longer than you inhale – When we inhale, we activate the sympathetic nervous system which is essentially our 'go' function and when we exhale we trigger the parasympathetic nervous system which is our 'stop' function. Therefore,

if we exhale longer than we inhale we give the body and brain an opportunity to feel safer and calmer for longer.

With this knowledge, we can therefore use the breath as a constant tool to help lower anxiety and anxious moments.

Know Your Triggers

If you have struggled with anxiety for a long time, you may feel that you have little or no idea why it shows up in your life. You may even be in a pattern of waking feeling anxious immediately before you have even begun to engage with the day ahead.

However, anxiety is not random, and your experience of anxiety will be triggered by different stimuli. When we feel that anxiety is random, it can be even more frightening, leaving us wondering if and when it will rear its ugly head once more but if we can recognise triggers in our life that lead to and add to anxiety, we will regain some control which in itself will lower our anxiety.

The next time you feel anxious, sit with it for a moment and ask yourself a series of questions (you can use the handout in our resources to make this easier for you).

Firstly, score your anxiety out of 10, of course this is subjective but it can help in order for you to get an indication of where it is in this moment.

Then ask yourself:

- Where am I? – Does your anxiety show up more in a particular place?

- Who am I with? – Are there certain people who make you feel more or less anxious when you are around them?

- What can I see? – Have you become anxious as you have seen something which has previously made you feel unsafe or has a familiarity to something that has made you feel unsafe?

- What can I hear? – Is there a certain song in the background or does the sound of the 10 o'clock news theme tune cause anxiety?

- What can I smell? – Our sense of smell is very powerful in causing us to evoke emotions and feelings, maybe the smell of petrol reminds you of a stressful car trip or a certain food smell triggers an anxious feeling?

- What can I taste? – Can you taste something right now? Does the taste of a certain food or drink bring up anxious feelings?

- What am I touching? – Are you physically touching something which is causing the anxiety, maybe the feel of a certain fabric?

- What am I feeling? – Asides from the obvious anxiety, are there other feelings and emotions going on? Do you feel sad, afraid, guilty etc?

- What thoughts am I having? –
  We tend to believe all of our
  thoughts and yet most of our
  thoughts are based upon pure
  conjecture and opinion and very
  few are based upon actual facts.
  Pay attention to your thoughts
  and notice what they are saying
  to you as if you were an observer
  of them.

- Is there anything making the
  anxiety worse? – Does it feel
  worse when you scroll social
  media? Speak to a certain
  person? Withdraw from people?

- What could make me feel better
  right now? – Do not look too far
  ahead, just in this moment, what
  could help you rather than hurt
  you? Maybe taking some slow
  deep breaths, going for a walk,
  calling a friend or even having a
  nap.

Whilst it may feel challenging to ask
yourself all of these questions, there are
multiple benefits to doing the exercise. It will
not only help you gain clarity and insight into

your own triggers but simply the act of doing the exercise will move your attention from your survival brain and into your calmer and more rational Prefrontal Cortex.

Manage Your Diet

We tend to always think of our diet as our food intake, but our diet is actually anything we consume. Whatever we consume, just like our food, accumulates to make us who we are and can make us healthy or unhealthy.

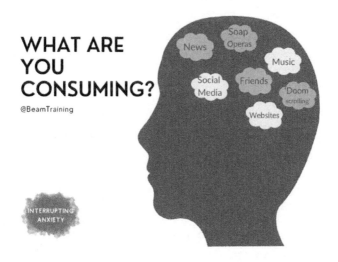

If you consider what you consume daily, you will begin to realise that you are a constant consumer of information. According to the Marketing and Media Research organisation Carat, we now consume 90 times more data than we did in 1940, meaning we are constantly consuming huge amounts of data that our ancestors did not have to deal with.

Whilst being informed and connected can of course be a positive side effect of this, there are also downfalls and negative consumption is one of them. We are now exposed to thousands of news channels, opinions, blogs, social media networks and advertising campaigns in a way that our great grandparents would have never been exposed to.

If this level of consumption was equated to food, it would be no wonder that we would all be feeling unhealthy and unhappy.

When we begin to pay attention to what we are consuming we can begin to recognise things that are good for us (e.g. certain friends or certain music) and also things that are making us anxious (e.g. watching the news late at night) and just as we would with food, begin to eliminate or at least reduce our intake of the things making us feel unhappy and anxious.

Go Green

We all know that exercise is good for our physical health but exercise gives us so much more than physical strength, in fact I would argue that exercise is more important for our mental health.

There are many research studies out there that look at the benefits of exercise and mental health. Several of those studies, specifically looked at if how we exercise is more beneficial to our mental health.

In fact, there is a term known as 'green exercise' which was coined by the University of Essex who have been studying the impact of outdoor exercise on our mental health since 2003.

What research has shown is that when we exercise outdoors, and especially in a natural green environment, we reap more benefits than if we exercise indoors. Some of the shown benefits are:

- Stress Levels Reduce – Amazingly even just looking at a natural green space begins to lower our stress hormones and make us feel calmer. This is a wonderful side effect for those of us who struggle with anxiety.

- Improved Mental Focus – When we exercise outdoors, we need to be more present with the environment as it changes. We have to be aware of altering terrain, weather changes and potential dangers causing us to be more in the present moment than when we exercise in a gym.

- Improves Vitamin D levels – Being outdoors allows us to increase our vitamin D levels through sunlight. Vitamin D deficiency has been linked to a wide range of physical health ailments but is increasingly linked to anxiety as well.

Key Takeaways

- We are able to lower our experience of anxiety with some simple tools.

- Talking to someone will give perspective but it is important you choose the right person to talk to. Alternatively, writing things down can also help.

- Our breath is a powerful tool available to us to reassure the brain that we are safe and lower anxiety.

- We can all be triggered by different stimuli when we experience anxiety and it is useful to start to identify some of our triggers.

- Our diet is more than what we eat, it is everything we consume some of which, can cause us to feel even more anxious.

- Outdoor exercise has been proven to be beneficial for us in many ways.

In the next chapter, you will learn...

Ways in which you can help someone else who may be struggling with anxiety.

Chapter Five: How to Help Someone With Anxiety

So far, when considering anxiety, we have predominantly considered how it impacts us, which is essential, we always need to help ourselves before we are in a position to truly help others.

However, you may be reading this considering a colleague, friend or loved one who you know is struggling with anxiety but you just do not know how to approach the topic with them nor do you know how you can help them.

When we see someone we care about struggling with their mental health in any way, it can be daunting, we can become fearful of saying the wrong thing and in doing so, often choose to say nothing. Most people who are struggling, will tell you that the worse thing anyone can say is nothing at all. It can cause the sufferer to feel even more isolated and stuck in their heads.

Let's now look at some ways in which we can become more confident and comfortable in supporting those people.

Be Proactive

If you are concerned about someone who may be experiencing difficulties with anxiety, approaching them in a caring way and offering support may make a huge difference to them, but it can also feel daunting to do so.

Proactively approach them; initiate a conversation with the person asking how they are feeling, whilst we can never force someone to open up, we can offer the space for them to do so by asking and genuinely listening to their replies.

When talking to the person, be sure to ask open ended questions like "What was your evening like?" Rather than "Did you have a nice evening?" this will encourage a more open dialogue rather than it being instantly closed down with yes or no responses.

Hearing isn't Listening

The challenge from initiating that initial conversation is that when someone does open up to us, we need to genuinely listen to their response.

Despite what we may think, most of us are really poor listeners and listen with the intent of replying causing us to miss out on what is really being said, we hear them but we do not always listen to them.

For example, you bump into a friend and ask how they are, they begin tell you they are tired from a heavy weekend and as they are talking you instantly start thinking about how you will tell them about what you did on the weekend too. However, whilst constructing your response and waiting for them to pause so you can jump in and tell them, you have entirely missed what they were trying to tell you.

The problem is, the second part of what your friend was telling you could have been something really revealing and you have missed it and / or missed an opportunity to delve a little further into why their weekend was heavy.

In therapy, we see this all the time and also see how most of us also expect those interactions to be fairly superficial. In fact, most of the time, we all offer 'stock' answers to every day questions such as "How are you?" which rarely reflect how we are really feeling.

When someone comes into the therapy room, as they settle in the therapist will usually ask how they are and regularly the client will respond with this 'stock' response that they have been telling everyone saying something like "yeah, I'm doing okay thanks". The truth is, the person is coming for therapy and so they undoubtedly have things they need to talk about but if the therapist took their response on face value, they may say "Oh great, well if you're doing ok, let's meet again in a month". Obviously, this would be a terrible way to support someone and run a therapy practice, so instead therapists will have learned ways to delve a little deeper.

One tool that I personally love to use, is something that I call practicing the pause. This tool is where you do not fill the silence when someone is talking and you leave space for them to elaborate on what they have already said. You do not need to make this uncomfortable, you can smile, ask another open question, make subtle agreement noises and nods, but you do not fill the space by distracting the conversation. The amazing part of practicing the pause, and I've learnt it without exception, not just in the therapy room, but in my personal relationships as well, is the second thing people tell you is more honest and revealing than the first.

The first response someone gives you is their rehearsed 'stock' phrase. That's what they're telling everyone. The second thing they tell you is what they tell you when they feel truly listened to.

You Don't Need to Fix Someone

When talking to someone who is trying to support a loved one, I have commonly heard them say "I just wish I knew how to fix it for them". It is an instinct so many of us share, we see someone struggling and suffering and our desire is to fix and resolve it straight away.

Very occasionally, something may be within our power to fix, but most of the time, we do not have the power to fix someone else's problems and certainly do not have the power to make someone feel happier or less anxious.

Whilst this may be difficult to accept, when we do accept that we do not have responsibility for fixing everything, we are in a better position to listen and support. I vividly remember a delegate asking a question on a course I was delivering, he said "When my wife gets home after a hard day and complains to me about all the things that have gone wrong, if I start to tell her what she needs to do to fix it, she gets angry at me. I am only trying to help."

Of course, everyone in the room understood that this person was just trying to help his wife, but many people also recognised that maybe the wife was not 'moaning' about things because she wanted them fixed, but maybe she just needed to feel heard, understood and wanted someone to be on her side.

When we stop putting responsibility on ourselves to fix other people's challenges, we become much more able to be present and supportive.

Respect Their Privacy

If someone has the courage to open up to you about how they are feeling, you are responsible for keeping that information safe with only two exceptions, if you believe that the person is a risk to themselves and / or others then you have a responsibility to get them the help they need by contacting a medical professional, but if you do find yourself in this situation, please do inform the person that this is what you will be doing.

However, most of the time, this is not the case and so if someone has trusted you with their private experience, I urge you to see this as a privilege and something that you will not abuse. That information should never be shared nor ever be held against them.

If you betray someone's trust when they open up to you about their mental health, it is not only likely they would never open up to you again but also possible that they may never open up to anyone again.

Key Takeaways

- Do not let your fear of saying the wrong thing, prevent you from saying anything.

- Most of us listen with the intent of replying, learn to practice the pause and become a better listener.

- Overcome the urge to try to fix a problem and focus upon being present and supportive instead.

- If somebody opens up to you, ensure you keep their trust.

In the next chapter, you will learn...

All about panic attacks and how to help yourself or someone else dealing with a panic attack.

Chapter Six: Panic Attacks

If you have anxiety, you may never have a panic attack, however there are of course some people who do suffer with anxiety which can also cause them to have panic attacks.

Panic attacks are horrible things to experience. I had helped people with panic attacks for about 10 years, yet I had never experienced one personally. Then, in 2019, my father died suddenly and unexpectedly, I was called out of the blue to his house and had to see my father dead when he had been alive and healthy moments before. Even on the day he died, I began to have panic attacks, I recall struggling to breathe and feeling as though I was about to throw up and pass out simultaneously. However, as the days and weeks went by, this got worse for me, and I had multiple panic attacks. Times where I felt my heart race, my vision blur and unable to breathe became a regular thing and all of a sudden, I had a new found understanding and respect for panic attacks and the people who suffer regularly with them.

Thankfully, with time, therapy and lots of the tools I will share with you here, I no longer suffer with them and hopefully my experience led me to being able to help others far better than I had before.

The Physical Symptoms of Panic Attacks

Panic attacks are a very physical experience, they can appear seemingly out of nowhere, and can build really quickly.

Unsurprisingly, when people experience panic attacks, they very often might think they are having a heart attack, because some of the characteristic symptoms of a panic attack are a pounding, racing heart and a tightness in the chest.

If you are experiencing a panic attack, you may have a whole combination of symptoms. You might feel as though you cannot catch your breath, you might feel dizzy, lightheaded, very hot, very cold, sick, you might even have a stabbing pain in your chest, which again, leads people to think they are having a heart attack. You may pull at your clothes as they feel suddenly constricting, you may feel like your legs are shaking, or turn into jelly. And you might have a sense of disassociation (you may know everyone's talking, but feel as though you are not really there, like you are watching it, but are not part of it).

Again, we can all have a different experience and not feel all these physical symptoms.

Why do we have panic attacks?

Amazingly, the reason we have a panic attack is to protect us, because stress and anxiety have built up so much in our body, that it is causing us harm. Causing our brain and our body to need to release some of the stress and anxiety right now (almost like loosening a lid to release some steam). Sometimes, this appears as an emotional outburst, crying or getting angry, but sometimes this can also appear as a panic attack. Therefore, in a way, it is a protective mechanism to release the huge amounts of stress we have stored.

Quite often, once the panic attack has calmed down and we go through feeling exhausted, we do feel a bit better.

A panic attack can be triggered by anything we feel hugely stressed by. In my personal example, the stress of losing my dad, but it could be the stress of being in a crowd of people or the stress of a big event.

What we do know, is that unfortunately, panic attacks can also be self fulfilling. Once someone experiences how horrible and unpleasant a panic attack is, sometimes the stress of fearing another panic attack is enough to keep causing them. The very thing we fear, is caused by us fearing it.

How to help ourselves or someone else with a panic attack

Yet again, there is no one size fits all for this, but there are some powerful ways in which you can help yourself and others if you notice a panic attack occurring. These will be more helpful at different stages of the panic attack so use your discernment.

Get Some Space

When we notice someone starting to have a panic attack, we may at first think they are just upset or feeling a bit panicky and what we will then often do is put our arm around someone or we might crowd them, this is usually a trigger for the person to feel more stressed and likely to amplify the panic attack.

Instead of touching them, offer support for example asking if they feel wobbly, say do they need some help to sit down on a chair. Unless they're in physical danger, give them space.

One of the best tools is get them outside if you can to give them that sense of space, if you cannot get them outside open a window, so that they can feel the fresh air and also look into the distance.

Move

A panic attack is a build up of energy, if they're able to, if they're not too dizzy and they don't feel faint, get them to walk around. If they cannot walk around, help them to release some of the energy by shaking, it can really help to shake out the hands or legs or even stomp the feet.

Stop Everything

You can offer words of reassurance but when having a panic attack, the brain has become overstimulated so it is helpful to try and create a calm and quiet environment, ask other people to step away, turn off music / tv if possible.

Focus On The Senses

This is a brilliant mindfulness tool which helps at times of panic and high anxiety. If we are feeling anxious, then we are preparing for an imminent threat. In order for us to reassure the brain that we are actually safe in the moment, we can use our senses to come back to the present moment with this exercise:

1) Find three things you can see and name them.

2) Find three things you can hear and name them.

3) Find three things you can touch and name them.

4) Find three things you can taste (even by imagination) and name them.

5) Find three things you can smell (even by imagination) and name them.

Ground Yourself

If you are an anxious person, there is a good chance you rarely have your whole foot connected to the floor. Interestingly, our feet tell our brain how we want to act next, if you sit with your feet on the tips of their toes, our brain interprets this as we may need to move quickly soon and that can make us feel more anxious and on edge.

A fantastically simple exercise that this is not just a panic attack, you can do this throughout the day, is practicing connecting both feet to the floor.

Sitting straight in a chair, lean forward as if you were going to stand up. Allow the legs to engage and start to put pressure down into your feet but do not stand up. Now settle back in your chair but keep your feet just as connected, feel the heels connected, the balls connected, the toes are connected, push down and keep that connection with your feet.

The simple but powerful part of that is it sends a signal to your brain saying that I'm safe, I'm not going to go anywhere. But also, when you do this exercise, you are not in your brain, you are in your feet.

Breathing

We have already learned how and why breathing is so impactful on reducing anxiety and how when we suffer with a panic attack, a common symptom is feeling as though we cannot breathe. It is therefore useful to focus upon the breath as soon as possible during a panic attack and try to encourage slower more controlled breaths in and out through the nose.

A common mistake when someone's having a panic attack, is to encourage them to take huge deep breaths, this can increase the stress so instead of that just focus on slowing the breathing down little by little.

Key Takeaways

- Panic attacks feel very physical and can have a whole range of symptoms.

- Panic attacks occur as our brain and body feels the build up of stress within us is too much, the panic attack protects us by releasing some of that stress.

- There are many ways in which we can help ourselves and / or others when having a panic attack but it is important to be sensitive to the person and do what helps them in the moment.

In the next chapter, you will learn...

As we conclude our book, we will take a quick review over what we have covered along with offering some further help and support resources if you need them.

Conclusion

Anxiety is such a broad experience, it is important that we understand that we can each experience it in slightly different ways, the main thing to recognise is that whilst suffering with anxiety can feel overwhelming and debilitating, there are lots of ways in which we can learn to lower our anxiety.

For many people, overcoming anxiety is just not a realistic outcome at this stage but the tools and exercises we have covered throughout this book are designed to help you regain control by recognising that you can interrupt anxiety.

Key tools you now have within your toolkit are:

- Understanding the benefit of talking to someone about how you feel.

- Knowing why breathing may be the most simple tool you have available to change your anxiety.

- Understanding your unique experience of anxiety by

understanding your own triggers and therefore being better able to manage them.

- Recognising the benefits of 'green exercise'.

We have also explored how we can support others who are anxious by not only applying our own tools where appropriate but by also:

- Being proactive in how we ask people how they are feeling.

- Being better listeners by practicing the pause.

- Understanding that we are not required to 'fix' anyone.

- Honouring privacy to create trust.

Finally, we looked at the impact of panic attacks, understanding that in a way, they are our brains way of protecting us from becoming overly stressed. This release, can be incredibly frightening for the sufferer but there are key ways in which we can help ourselves and / or others:

- Create space and be sure not to overcrowd the person.

- Encourage them to move where possible, even if only shaking their hands.

- Stop all unnecessary sensory stimulation.

- By using the senses, we can distract the brain and bring it back to the present moment.

- Grounding our feet helps to calm the brain.

- Breathing is again crucial and should be encouraged to be slow and calm.

Whether you are struggling or a loved one, it is reassuring to know that you are certainly not alone and if we are able to keep growing our toolkit, we do not have to let anxiety ruin or rule our life.

If you feel that your anxiety is not manageable with these tools and techniques, then I urge you to speak to a professional about other possible ways you can receive help and support.

Further Help & Support

Of course, you can speak with your GP but there are also other wonderful charities and networks out there who also offer great help and may be able to offer additional or supplementary support to the NHS. Here are a few I would recommend.

Anxiety UK (www.anxietyuk.org.uk) Anxiety UK has both national and international reach to offer help and support to anyone suffering with anxiety or an anxiety related condition. They have been around for over 50 years and have a whole wealth of knowledge and resources.

No Panic (www.nopanic.org.uk) Have a fantastic helpline for adults (0300 772 9844) and also a dedicated helpline for young people (0333 772 2644) which is open 365 days a year 10am until 10pm. They urge people not to suffer alone and to contact them if they are struggling.

OCD Action (www.ocdaction.org.uk) OCD Action help people understand Obsessive Compulsive Disorder better as well as offering support to those struggling with it.

MIND (www.mind.org.uk) not just for anxiety, MIND offer support and resources for people struggling with a wide array of mental health issues. They also have some local centres to offer help with housing, accessing support, training and employment.

Mental Health Resources at Work. If you are employed, find out what mental health resources are available from your employers, some offer Employee Assistance Programmes where you can access free counselling and support, some may have help groups or run workshops.

Further Resources & Recommended Reading

- Bernhardt, Klaus (2018) The Anxiety Cure: Live a Life Free From Panic in Just a Few Weeks

- McGee, Paul (2012) How Not To Worry: The Remarkable Truth of How a Small Change Can Help You Stress Less and Enjoy Life More

- McKeown, Patrick (2020) The Oxygen Advantage

- Green Exercise | University of Essex (https://www.essex.ac.uk/researc h-projects/green-exercise)

- What are anxiety disorders? - Mind (https://www.mind.org.uk/informat ion-support/types-of-mental-health-problems/anxiety-and-panic-attacks/anxiety-disorders/)

Worksheets & Resources

You can access further resources and downloads on our website here:

https://www.beamtraining.co.uk/beamresources

Anxiety Checklist

Date

Out of 10 how intense is the anxiety	What thoughts am I having?
Where am I?	
Who am I with?	
What can I see?	Is there anything making the anxiety worse?
What can I hear?	
What can I smell?	
What can I taste?	What could make me feel better right now?
What am I touching?	
What am I feeling?	

INTERRUPTING ANXIETY

www.beamtraining.co.uk

Acknowledgments

This book is the result of many years writing and delivering courses, workshops and coaching schedules for the thousands of clients and delegates I have worked with.

It has been my experience that no matter what issue a client has presented to me, be it a relationship problem, a phobia, a lack of confidence etc. there is always an element of anxiety present. Over the years, I have learned very simple tools which have helped to lower that anxiety for people (and myself!) and so would like to thank every single one of those clients and delegates for being so open, honest and courageous in sharing their challenges with me.

During my career, it has often been assumed that whilst I teach about confidence, happiness, being calm, being relaxed, that I must never experience the opposite. This is not the case! I have struggled with periods of anxiety throughout my life, much of which I had never even named, and had put a lot of my energy into concealing from others for fear of judgement.

It is only with the help and support of my husband, Tom, that this has come to light, and this has been something I too have consistently worked on. I am filled with gratitude for his love, support, patience and understanding.

I also must acknowledge the tremendous teachings my daughter has given me, she is without doubt my greatest teacher in this life; challenging me, loving me, helping me always want to be a better version of myself. Her ability to show wisdom beyond her years has always astounded and reassured me.

Finally, I thank you, there are countless books out there and to settle in and read any is a commitment of your precious time, the fact that you have read this is humbling. Thank you.

About the Author

Lianne Weaver is an author, speaker, trainer and therapeutic coach with more than a decade of experience working within wellbeing and personal development.

After gaining a BA (Hons) Education whilst specialising in psychology, Lianne dreamed of becoming a play therapist. Despite completing the course to do so, her personal circumstances meant she needed to find employment quickly after her qualifying and so she began work within a call centre at a financial institution. Quickly, she was promoted into Human Resources where she was then sponsored to do a Post Grad in Human Resource Management which she really enjoyed.

However, shortly after qualifying, she discovered she was pregnant and knew she would need to put her career aside to care for her daughter. As time went by, returning to a career in HR seemed more and more unlikely and after several diversions, Lianne decided to retrain as a bookkeeper. She did so and began preparing people's books from home whilst she continued studying as an Accounting Technician (AAT).

As her daughter began school, Lianne set up a bookkeeping and accountancy practice which created an illusion of success all around her. However, internally, Lianne felt unhappy, lost and afraid. She had realised she was in a life she did not like nor was healthy for her and yet felt unable to make any changes.

Eventually, in 2010, Lianne essentially left her life with her daughter, her dog and very little money. In essence she had to start her life all over again and struggled with this until she decided to venture into studying holistic therapies. She took courses on Reiki, Aromatherapy, Massage and more and started a small holistic therapy practice. Here, she met many interesting people and was invited to speak at an organisation who subsequently asked if she could deliver a training programme on wellbeing.

Since that time, Lianne has created over 100 courses on topics ranging from stress to forgiveness to meditation and much more, most of which are CPD accredited. She has continued to learn and moved into talking therapies such as Emotional Freedom Technique (EFT), Neuro-Linguistic Programming (NLP), Coaching and Havening. Her business, Beam Development & Training Ltd, now delivers wellbeing and personal development training in organisations around the world and she still enjoys working with clients on a one to one basis as a Therapeutic Coach when she is able.

Lianne has worked as a wellbeing and personal development expert for large organisations, been on many international podcasts and has spoken on stages as a leader in her field.

In her free time, Lianne lives with her husband Tom and dog Dave and enjoys nothing more than being with her family, especially her daughter.

Online Content

For further resources please visit https://www.beamtraining.co.uk/beamresource s or scan the QR code below.

Printed in Great Britain
by Amazon

21938316R00050